I will show you,
HOW YOU CAN PLAY BETTER GOLF

I will show you,
HOW YOU CAN PLAY BETTER GOLF

John Oteri
Photographs by Frank Curran.

COPYRIGHT © 2012 BY JOHN OTERI.

LIBRARY OF CONGRESS CONTROL NUMBER:		2011919685
ISBN:	HARDCOVER	978-1-4653-9008-0
	SOFTCOVER	978-1-4653-9007-3
	EBOOK	978-1-4653-9009-7

All rights reserved. No part of this book may be reproduced or transmitted in any form or by any means, electronic or mechanical, including photocopying, recording, or by any information storage and retrieval system, without permission in writing from the copyright owner.

Photographs by Frank Curran
www.frankcurranphoto.com or mail to: frank@frankcurranphoto.com

Edited by Richard Oteri

This book was printed in the United States of America.

To order additional copies of this book, contact:
Xlibris Corporation
1-888-795-4274
www.Xlibris.com
Orders@Xlibris.com

CONTENTS

About the Author 9
Endorsements 11
Introduction 13

Section 1

Golf Fitness 17
Warm Up Before Play 18
Your Golf Equipment 19
Clean Equipment 20
Hybrid Clubs 21
Play By the Rules 22

Section 2

The Golf Grip 25
Alignment 35
Posture 38
The Pre Shot Routine 39
Visualization 40

Section 3

Putting, Grip, Stance, Stroke 43
Putting—Distance Control 54
The Short Putt 56
The Hybrid Putt 57
Reading Greens 58

Section 4

The Short Game 63
Pitch from a Tight Lie 64
The Short Pitch 65
Chipping 66
The Bump and Run 71
Bunker Play—the Fried Egg 73
Bunker Play 74

Section 5

Select the Right Club 85
Use The Right Wedge 86
One-Arm Drill 87
Creating Backspin 88
The Flop Shot 89
Play From Green Side Rough 90
Playing From Hard Pan 92

Section 6

Saving Strokes 97
Play To the Middle of the Green 98
The Par Threes 99
Uneven Lies 100

Section 7

The Driver 105
The Takeaway 110
The Impact Zone 114
Clubhead Lag 116
Transition—Back To Down 119
The Long Irons 120
Golf And Baseball 121
Swing Through To The Finish 122

SECTION 8

The Quick Hook 125
The Draw 126
The Slice 127
The Fade 128
The Topped Shot 129
Split Grip 130

SECTION 9

Purposeful Practice 133
Drive It Low 135
Hit It Low From the Fairway 136
The Release 137
Right Knee Flex 138
A Higher Ball Flight 139
Get an Overhaul 140

John Oteri has been a PGA Professional in the New England Section for the past 53 years. He has served as Head Golf Professional at Blue Hill Country Club in Canton, Massachusetts, Thorny Lea Golf Club in Brockton, Massachusetts, and at Strawberry Valley Golf Club in Abington, Massachusetts.

Mr. Oteri is currently teaching at Poquoy Brook Golf Club in Lakeville, Massachusetts. He is also teaching at the Charlie Lanzetta Junior Golf School in Rockland, Massachusetts; voted the #1 Junior Golf School in the United States in 2001.

Endorsements

Johnny O is one of the finest and most knowledgeable golf professionals I have ever been fortunate enough to meet. His expertise, easy to understand communication style and his thorough understanding of the golf swing make him an extremely respected instructor among players of all skill levels. Ever since I was a 12 year old and winning junior tournaments all over New England, I always said Johnny O is my pro and Johnny O should be your pro too.

John Van Wart, Professional Golfer

My first introduction to John was via a lesson I was having with another pro. This was our club pro with whom I had played many rounds of golf, taken lessons with, liked and admired. One day he was especially frustrated with my inability to make a more upright swing. John happened to be near the practice tee and being a friend of our club pro was called over by him to take a look. I had heard about John, and more importantly, that he had taught some of the best players in the state. In a very soft voice that only I could hear, John asked me to strengthen my right hand slightly on the club. He asked me how it felt. He asked me to hit some balls. He told me he did not think my swing was that bad. I remember hitting the ball solidly and with confidence. After that I went back to John many times to learn more secrets of the game.

Nowadays I live far from John but still use the techniques he taught me in both the short game and the full swing. The only thing I miss is not having John to turn to when I need help.

John Follett, Hawkinsville, GA

I started going to John Oteri for golf lessons two years ago. I was having trouble hooking the ball and could not figure out why. I had been to a golf pro before for help with my swing and the first thing they wanted to do was tear apart my swing and start over. That's the great thing about Oteri, he has been around the game for a long time and knows everything there is to know about the golf swing. He made some minor adjustments and in no time I was hitting the ball much straighter and further. That's when I knew he was the real deal. I went from a 5 handicap to a +1 handicap in a matter of months. Later that season I won my club championship along with four other tournaments and I owe it all to John Oteri,

Tim Johnson, Lakeville, MA

John Oteri, my golf instructor and mentor, has had a profound influence on my golf game. He is a gifted teacher, patient yet strong in his style. John took me from being a rank beginner to a respectable golfer within 2 seasons of taking lessons with him. His love for the game is evident, his knowledge is vast. Having his words of wisdom in print will be an indispensable resource for every golfer.

Jayne Gallimore, Lakeville, MA

Time and time again I have seen PGA teaching pro "Johnny O" turn someone's game around with an easily learned and applied adjustment to their game. He is amazing in how he can suggest a minor adjustment for an immediate remedy that will impact your golf game. I have taken many strokes off my game with a simple repositioning of the hands that gave me more hit and much more height for those soft landing iron shots.

Ken Murphy, Orlando, FL

I met John Oteri in 1991 when he was the head Golf Pro at Thorny Lea Golf Club in Brockton, MA. I decided to take golf seriously and took 5 lessons with John; over the course of 10 weeks that season my handicap went from a 22 to 15. That same year I won most improved golfer of the year at Thorny Lea.

Bob Berks, Canton, MA

John Oteri, PGA Professional, has been a key instructor for our Junior Golf Program at Rockland Golf Course for several years. His teaching techniques are excellent and the manner in which he communicates to each one of our students is very professional. His knowledge of the fundamentals of the golf swing and the game of golf is demonstrated with every lesson that John teaches. His thoughts, words, and especially his actions are one of a true professional.

Charlie Lanzetta, PGA Golf Professional

Introduction

As a golf instructor for over fifty years and working with thousands of golfers of all levels, I came to realize that they all could play better golf.

The three ingredients they all need are good basic fundamentals, the technique needed to play various shots, and the willingness to practice.

Golf is an art, not a science. When you watch the tour players of today and see great looking golf swings such as Ernie Els and Luke Donald and not-so-great in Jim Furyk and Bubba Watson those four swings cannot be copied. What they all have at impact is the clubface square to the target. How they got there is immaterial. In this book you will not find secret moves to a great golf swing or numerous golf swing theories but instead easy to understand simple practical advice. Simple changes in setup, and ball position are the keys to success in making the shot.

The one area of the game that one must attempt to master is the short game—the range from one hundred yards and into the cup. These short shots—the critical shots that lead to lower scores are what most amateurs are lacking. A player with a good long game but poor short game has no advantage over a player with a good short game. Most of the strokes compiled in a round of golf are played around the greens. I do not see many amateurs spending quality time chipping, pitching, and putting. Your game will improve when you put more emphasis into the short game. I recommend that you practice 80 percent on the short game and 20 percent on the long game.

By developing sound fundamentals, the techniques to playing various golf shots and knowing how and what to practice is the only way to improve your scores. When you look at the world's best players, you see great golf shots made with different-looking swings. The key to great ball striking is at the moment of impact, the club head meeting the ball. The pros do it and they all do it their own way. There are several factors to consider such as but not limited to age, flexibility, height, weight, overall strength,

JOHN OTERI

and hand-eye coordination. Can you imagine anyone attempting to copy the swings of Tiger Woods, Jim Furyk, Ernie Els, Fred Couples, or Bubba Watsons?

It is not necessary to have a perfectly good-looking swing to play better golf. Develop good basics, and do it your way.

John Oteri

SECTION 1

Golf Fitness	17
Warm Up Before Play	18
Your Golf Equipment	19
Clean Equipment	20
Hybrid Clubs	21
Play By the Rules	22

Golf Fitness

Golf is an athletic endeavor and requires dynamic movement throughout the swing. A lack of flexibility will result in loss of clubhead speed limiting ones ability to swing the club correctly. As we age, we are certain to lose flexibility along with muscle loss. However, no matter what age you may be, you are able to slow this process to some degree with a golf flexibility program.

Flexibility is a key component to your overall swing. Before getting into a program, be sure to get approval from your physician.

If you have a passion for golf and wish to play better. Before you tee it up, add a ten-minute stretching program to your pre-shot routine.

The width of one's stance may be determined by your flexibility and swing tempo. If your flexibility is limited, then a narrower stance is recommended. If you have good flexibility and a fast tempo to your swing, then a wider stance is recommended.

Warm Up Before Play

Before playing, a round of golf is not the time to get serious about swing thoughts or trying the latest golf tips you just saw on the golf channel. It's too late, and it's time to just loosen up, go with the swing you have, and play golf.

A warm up session should start with a few minutes of stretching and swinging a weighted club. Once you have limbered up, hit some pitch shots, and work your way up to the driver.

Before leaving the range, play an imaginary golf hole. Hit the drive, then a fairway wood or iron to a target. Step over to the practice green, and hit a chip or two; a few putts and you are ready to go.

Your Golf Equipment

Playing with the wrong equipment is a major factor in a player being limited when it comes to improving one's ball striking. I compare it to wearing a pair of shoes that don't quite fit. They may work well for a short walk but cause big trouble down the road.

Golf clubs are designed for three-player ability levels for both men and women: the high handicap or novice, the mid handicap, and low handicap or expert player. There are many factors that contribute to putting the right set of clubs in the right pair of hands.

The main components to consider in the set are the *length*—lie of the clubhead in relation to the shaft—the *shaft flex*, and *overall weight*. A professional club fitter will consider the following issues when advising the right set for you.

- o   Your height—in most cases a standard length would do.
- o   The lie of the club—a club that is set too upright for the player will tend to hook.
- o   A club too flat will tend to slice.
- o   The shaft flex is determined by swing speed.
     Fast swing speed—stiff flex
     Slower speed—regular flex
     Slow speed—senior flex

There you have a general idea to club fitting.

In most cases you will get the opportunity to try a demo set on the golf course. Try before you buy is always a good policy.

If you are serious about your game, see your local PGA professional for help.

Clean Equipment

In many cases, I have students who come for instructions with dirty clubs. When the grooves on the clubface are full of grass and soil, the ball will not have enough backspin to carry into the air. Soiled grips are also an issue. Washing with hot water and wringing dry with a towel will bring back its natural tackiness. If you play more than two rounds a week, you should replace the grips each year.

Hybrid Clubs

The hybrid clubs are a combination of wood and iron that aid in a higher ball flight, replacing the more difficult to handle long irons. The clubs feature a compact head, a wide sole, and a low center of gravity. As a result of this design, the hybrids have replaced the 2, 3, 4, and in some cases the 5-iron from what you might call a conventional set of clubs. The hybrid club has contributed to lower scores by both professional and amateur golfers alike. The club is very effective from the rough, fairway bunkers, and for various shots around the greens.

I highly recommend adding one or two to your set.

Play By the Rules

The rules of golf can be confusing and complicated. They are, however, not intended to punish but to help players avoid penalties. No doubt many who play the game fudge on the rules intentionally and unintentionally. All serious players are obligated to protect their fellow competitors by knowing and playing by the rules.

Get yourself a rule book, know the basic rules, and have more fun playing the game.

SECTION 2

The Golf Grip 25
Alignment 35
Posture 38
The Pre Shot Routine 39
Visualization 40

The Golf Grip

A sound grip will help control the club in relation to the body rotation, allowing hands and body to work together. It is important that the club be held more in the fingers than in the palms. Only in this grip can you use the wrists—a power source—properly. Get into the habit of taking the grip very carefully each and every time. Before setting your hands on the club, be sure that the clubface is to the target and the grooves on the clubface are at a right angle to that line. To execute a proper left hand grip or forward hand follow these instructions:

- o The grip of the club will run from the middle of your index finger on a diagonal line to just under your little finger. You will hold the club in fingers and palm.
- o Looking down at the back of the hand with a so-called *neutral grip*, you will have one or two knuckles visible.
- o The thumb will lie on the top right quarter of the grip and the V shape between the thumb and first finger will point between the right ear and shoulder.

The *right hand* or rear hand is the power hand when working together with the left or forward hand. The hands want to be set facing each other and parallel with the right hand below the left.

- o This is a finger grip with the palm of the right hand covering the left thumb.
- o The grip of the club will set in the middle of the first finger with the feel of a trigger finger.
- o The left thumb will lie along the lifeline of the right hand.
- o An interlocking grip will have the little finger of the right interlocked with the first finger of the left.
- o The Vardon or overlap grip (first used by the great English player) will have the little finger of the right hand just overlap the first finger of the left.

- o The overlap grip is the most popular among the better players. However, Tiger Woods and Jack Nicklaus do use the interlock grip.
- o A full finger or baseball type grip may also be used and at times recommended.

Grip Pressure

- o The club should be held softly in the hands. On a pressure scale from 1-10; five or six will do.
- o A tight grip will restrict the arms and wrists from releasing properly.
- o Be aware that the grip may be the most important component of your golf swing.

You will rarely see a good player with a bad grip. You will, however, see bad players with bad grips.

The Grip (right handed player)

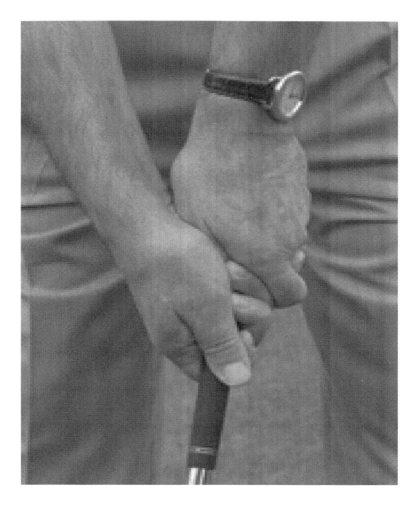

A **Neutral grip** will have the lines between the thumbs and first fingers pointing to the right shoulder and two knuckles showing on the top hand.

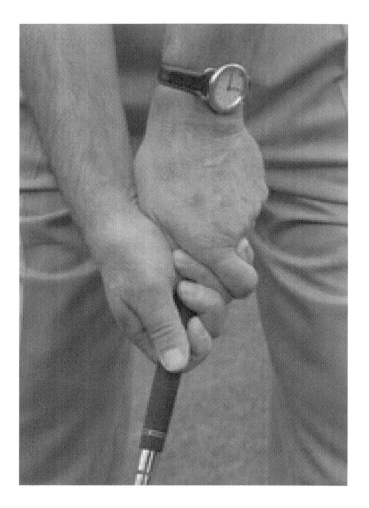

A **strong or hook grip** will have the lines between the thumbs and first fingers pointing to the right of the right shoulder and showing three knuckles on the top hand. This grip may be advised to limit a slice.

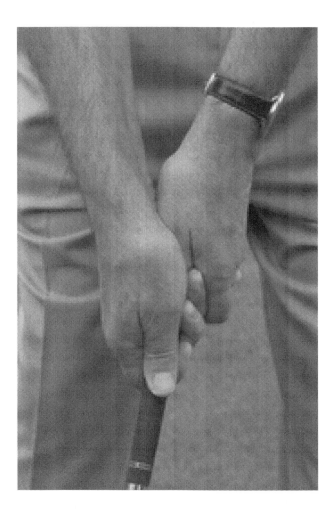

A **weak grip** will have the lines between the thumbs and the first fingers pointing at the chin and one knuckle showing on the top hand. This grip may be advised to limit a hook.

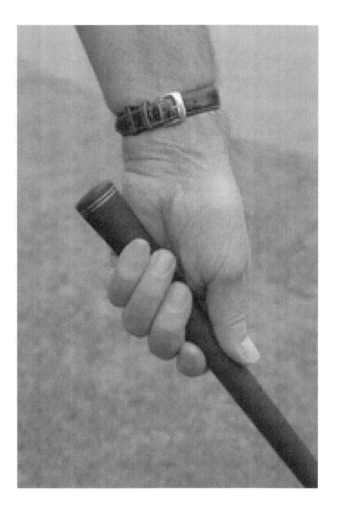

The left hand holds the club with a combination of the palm and fingers. The heel pad of the hand must be on top of the club.

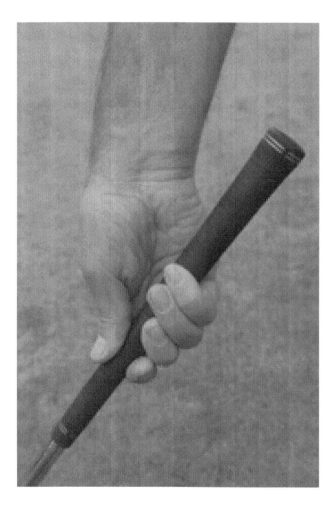

The grip of the club will set in the middle of the fingers. The palm of the right hand will cover the left thumb.

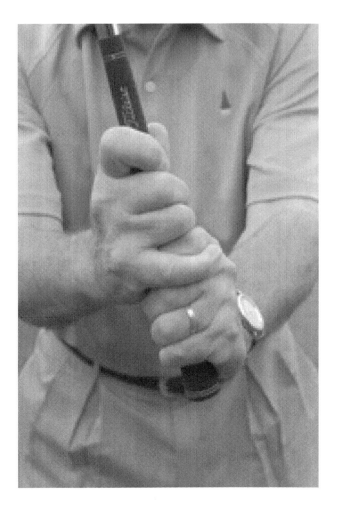

The **overlap or Vardon grip** (Invented by the British legend Harry Vardon) is the most widely used amongst the world's top players.

The **interlock grip** has the little finger of the right hand interlocking with the first finger of the left. Jack Nicklaus and Tiger Woods, two of the world's best players favored this grip.

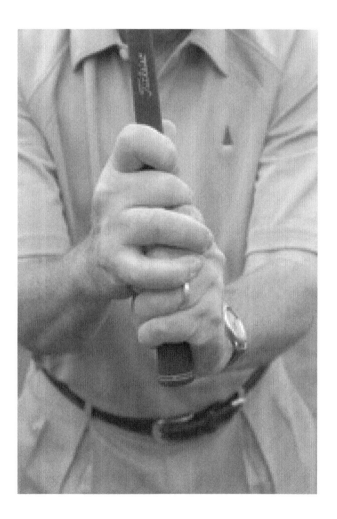

The **double overlap grip** is used by Jim Furyk who feels that with this grip he can keep the hook under control.

Alignment

Poor alignment or aim to the target is a major cause of misdirected shots. Before hitting any shot from a driver to a putter, your alignment to the target is your number one issue.

Follow these steps in your pre shot routine to proper alignment:

o   Face the target from behind the ball, and pick an intermediate spot on the target line, blade of grass, a divot, etc., a foot or two in front of the ball.
o   Sole the club at a right angle to the intended line with the grooves in the clubface straight back toward you.
o   Always set the club first, and then align your body to the target.
o   Bend from the hips and when setting your feet to the desired width, keep your heels parallel to the intended line. The knees and hips should also be parallel to the target line.
o   With the left foot turned out slightly to the target, it may appear that the stance is open.
o   The shoulders may be opened slightly and your eyes parallel to the intended line.
o   Always practice with directional guides to enforce the alignment procedure.
o   From this position, before starting the swing, look to the target by tilting your head while keeping your eyes parallel to the target line.
o   Picture the desired ball flight and make the swing.

To improve your alignment to the target, use guidelines (above). Be aware that your heel line is the true line to your target. This picture shows the player in a great set-up and posture. Notice the shoulder tilt, the Y shape with arms and the shaft tilted forward.

In a great set up as you see here, you want the lower back to feel concaved, bend from the hips, arms relaxed hanging straight down and the shaft of the club pointing to the belt line.

Posture

The definition of posture is the way a person holds himself. An example would be a model posing.

When setting up to hit a golf shot, one should be set in good posture. A player who comes to mind with great posture is Luke Donald. His setup is solid.

Steps to a Good Posture

- Set up without club, and stand erect.
- Bend from the hips. Don't slouch. Hang your arms straight down, totally relaxed.
- Push your buttocks out, and feel that your lower back is in a concave position.
- At this point, your fingertips will point at the tips of your toes and your knees over the shoelaces.

With this correct posture, you will increase your ability to be more consistent in your ball striking.

The Pre Shot Routine

The pre shot routine is simply preparing yourself to make the shot you are facing. When you watch tour players, you notice that they have the same approach before making any and all golf shots. Consistency is the name of the game, so develop and stay with a routine that works for you.

Visualization

When you step on the first tee, it is time to play golf. This is not practice where you think of a number of swing thoughts and how to improve on each. It is time, to trust the swing you have developed and allow your subconscious to kick in.

The great players in the game have vivid imaginations and know the result of a particular shot before the shot is played. It is just as easy to envision a positive picture as a negative one. Great players, Hogan, Nicklaus, Palmer, and Woods, I feel could, at times, will the ball into the cup. Raymond Floyd, who did not have what you would call a great looking swing, felt that the game of golf was 90 percent mental.

The body reacts to what the mind tells it to do. Visualization allows the subconscious to do its work. So think positive, and give it a go.

SECTION 3

Putting, Grip, Stance, Stroke 43
Putting—Distance Control 54
The Short Putt 56
The Hybrid Putt 57
Reading Greens 58

Putting, Grip, Stance, Stroke

There is no right way to grip the putter. The only right way to hold the putter is one that allows the putter to be square at impact.

A basic putting grip would have the following:

o   The grip of the putter running along the lifeline of both hands. One hand above the other with both thumbs running straight down the grip.
o   The palms in this case are parallel to one another and also parallel to the clubface.
o   Grip pressure from 1-10 would be at 5; that's it!

The Stance

o   A square stance is recommended with feet, hips, shoulders, and eyes parallel to the intended line.
o   Bend from the waist with a slight knee flex and the feet comfortably set apart.
o   Your eyes want to be over the heel of the clubhead, not the ball.
o   The forearms must be in line with the club.

The Stroke

The *putting stroke* is a golf swing that moves on an arc inside to square to inside. The stroke—not a hit at the ball—must be smooth with hands, arms, and shoulders moving in unison around a steady spine. The lower body remains still as the upper body rotates, and the upper arms stay connected to the body as they were in the address position. I recommend working with a putting guide that has an inside to inside putting track.

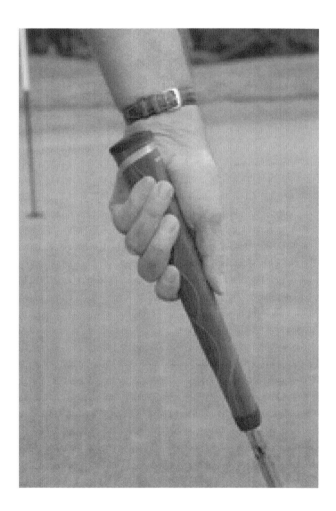

When using a conventional grip set the putter grip along the life line and in line with the forearm.

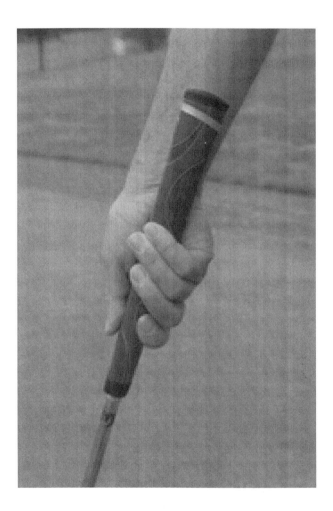

The right hand also has the club set along the life line.

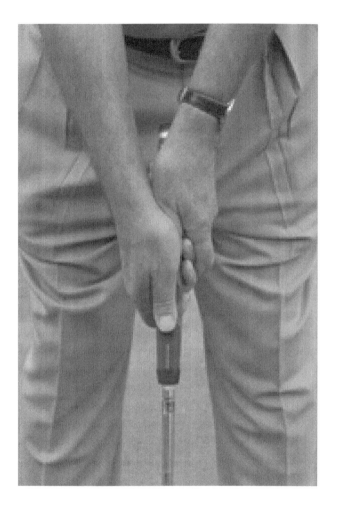

This putting grip will have the thumbs straight down the shaft with the palm of the right hand square to the intended line.

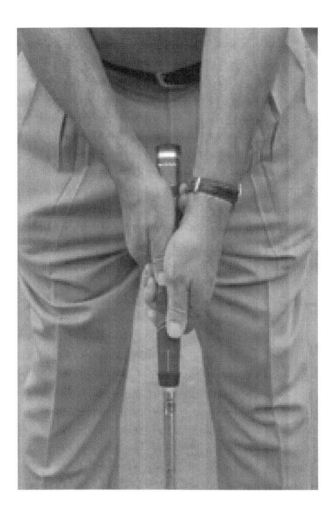

The left hand low or cross handed grip will help those players who have difficulty in keeping the left wrist from cupping at impact.

In this set-up you have feet, knees, hips and shoulders parallel to the target line. Note that the arms and club are in line and the eyes are over the heel of the putter not the ball.

Try this drill blocking the cup with tees giving you a smaller target to focus on.

I recommend practicing with a putting guide that promotes an inside to inside stroke. The guide above also allows you to practice keeping the putter head square through the ball.

To improve your stroke you want the upper arms to stay connected to your body back and through the stroke. In this photo the player placed a golf glove under each arm allowing him to make solid contact with the ball.

The one arm drill making several one arm puts. One arm and then the other is great practice for keeping the wrists firm back and through the stroke.

Try this drill made famous by Phil Michelson. Make all six in a row. I hope you are not in a hurry because this is a tough one!

Putting—Distance Control

The key to good putting is to eliminate the dreaded three-putt and to make most of the putts inside ten feet.

The computer we have, our brain, sees the distance through the eyes, and we perform the task so trust what you see.

Points to Consider When Practicing Distance Control

- Variables such as water, grain, the type of grass, and wind may come into play and affect the speed of the green.
- Spend most of your practice from ten feet in, starting from a foot or two and working back to the ten-foot range making five or ten putts in a row from each position.
- As putts get longer, the odds of making the putt diminish rapidly. Picture the longer putts as rolling into a cup four feet in diameter. If you miss, you are left with a two-foot putt. Not bad and no three-putts.
- When faced with a downhill shot from just off the green and the ball sitting in a decent lie, you will have much better distance control putting rather than chipping.
- There are times when your ball comes to rest on the fringe and against the first cut of ruff. When this happens it is sometimes easier to belly a wedge than to get a clean stroke on it with the putter. Select the sand wedge and use your normal putting set up. Stroke it half way up on the ball and it will roll like a putt.

With a ball just off the fringe, backed to the collar of the first cut of rough, using the sand iron as a putter is the way to go.

The Short Putt

There is nothing more frustrating, in my view, as having difficulty with the short putts. Many a player has walked away from the game due to this affliction. There are many reasons for missing "the short ones," and in some cases, it is mental. If you say, "I'm a bad putter," then you are a bad putter.

Let's look at some positive points that may lead to better putting.

- First and foremost, spend 90 percent of your practice putting inside ten feet.
- Select a putter that looks and feels good with the correct length and lie.
- Don't add pressure by feeling that you must make the putt. Your best putting is no doubt on the putting green where you are just practicing. When on the course try to develop the same attitude where you are relaxed and not "having to make the putt".
- When putting "the short ones," play the break off the center of the cup. Most players make the mistake of playing a two-inch break two inches outside the cup. With the cup's diameter 4 1/4 inches, a two inch break to a putt should be played inside the cup not two inches outside.
- Aim the name or line on the ball to the intended line. A ball starting on line with the right distance has a chance to go in. A putt that starts off line has zero chance of going in.
- Making a firmer stroke will eliminate some of the break-in shorter putts.
- Don't delay over the putt. Get into a routine where you picture the ball rolling into the cup; look back to the ball and go.
- With this positive picture, you will build a repeatable rhythm and tempo, and make more short ones.

If putting bugs you and you just keep missing from inside ten feet, then change what you are doing. Try a new grip or the belly putter which is in wide use on the PGA Tour.

The Hybrid Putt

Many amateurs with a weak chipping game would rather putt than chip from the greens edge.

For *better results*, try the *hybrid*:

- The putter has three to five degrees of loft where a hybrid 4-or 5-wood has fifteen to twenty degrees of loft. This extra loft and low center of gravity makes it easy to pop the ball onto the green, avoiding the uncertainty of rolling the putt through the fringe.

Setup and the Stroke

- Shorten down to the base of the grip and grip it as you would for a putt.
- Set the ball left of center with a slightly opened stance keeping your weight left.
- Keep your head still, and swing the club back and through low (no hinging of the wrists) allowing the loft to lift the ball onto the green,

Reading Greens

Following a routine is essential to building confidence and will lead to better putting.

Consider the following:

- As you approach the green, when possible, note how chip and pitch shots react as they roll out.
- As a rule, dark greens will roll slower than light-colored greens. A slow green will call for allowing more break; a fast rolling green, less break.
- When reading a putt, look from behind the ball, from what you believe is the low side of the break and at midpoint.
- Your initial assessment of the line is usually the correct one, so trust it, don't over-read the break.
- Be sure of the line since a ball that starts off line has little chance of being holed.
- Pick an intermediate target, an inch or two in front of the ball.
- A putt that comes up short and on line did have a chance to be holed. You want missed putts to settle a foot or so beyond the cup.
- The odds of making long putts are slim. Concentrate on distance.
- Every putt is a straight putt. Speed and gravity determine the break.
- Most missed putts from inside ten feet miss on the low side. With that in mind be firmer with the putt or play more break.
- When faced with a fast downhill putt, for better control of the speed, play the ball off the toe of the putter.
- The great putters make the short ones. Most of your practice putting should be inside ten feet.

Give Birdie Putts a Chance

When facing a birdie putt, the number one issue you face is to get the ball on the correct line and enough speed to reach the cup. Most amateurs will not average one birdie per round, and in most cases, leaving the ball short is the main reason. When facing a birdie putt, picture the cup eighteen inches beyond where it sits and focus on getting the ball to that spot. With this routine in mind, you will make those elusive birdies.

Practice Putting Blind

A great drill for making the three and four footers is to putt with your eyes closed. With your eyes closed, you get a great feel for the correct stroke. With your eyes closed, you will keep your head still, and no need to look up to see the ball. Feel the stroke; be aware of how the shoulders, arms, and hands are working together as one and not a hit at the ball. Stroke it and listen for the ball to drop.

SECTION 4

The Short Game	63
Pitch from a Tight Lie	64
The Short Pitch	65
Chipping	66
The Bump and Run	71
Bunker Play—the Fried Egg	73
Bunker Play	74

The Short Game

The short game, from one hundred yards into the hole, is where the winners separate from the losers.

The world's best players will hit no more than 60 to 70 percent of the greens in regulation. Therefore, they must get "up and down" in order to score. The average golfer finds chipping and pitching to be rather boring and spends most of his or hers allotted practice on the long game. The long game cannot help the short game, but the short game can help the long game. You will find it easier to make the proper corrections in the smaller swings that will lead to better swings in the long game.

If you are serious about improving your overall game, then I recommend the following:

An hour practice session.

50 minutes—chip, pitch and putt
10 minutes—long game

Pitch from a Tight Lie

A pitch shot from a tight lie to a difficult pin placement is a tough shot for the average player and advanced players alike. Every so often, this shot will be chunked, topped, or sculled across the green by the best of them. As part of your routine, consider all of your options, such as;

- Do I play to the tight pin placement or a spot on the green that affords me more room for error?
- Can I clear the bunker and still stay on the green?
- If I hit it thin, will it roll into the hazard?
- Always play the odds in your favor. Don't play shots you have little chance of making.

The Setup

- Select a club with less flange such as a pitching wedge. When using any club, you must, in the setup, sole the club with the hands ahead to eliminate the bounce effect.
- Take a narrow open stance, standing a bit closer to the ball with most of the weight on the forward foot.
- Shorten down on the club an inch or two position the ball in the center of your stance and keep the hands forward.
- Take a weak grip with the club soled and square to the target. An open clubface will add unwanted bounce to the sole of the club.
- This swing will be basically an upper body, hands, and arms swing with the lower body passive with little weight transfer
- The length of the swing will determine the distance.
- Swing the club down pinching the ball against the soil.

The Short Pitch

The short pitch shot is one of if not the most difficult shot for the average golfer. This shot requires feel and touch to carry the ball to the desired length and have it set quickly on the green. Hitting fat, chunked, or skulled shots in many cases is due to a poor setup, an improper weight transfer, and a scooping action through impact., To hit this shot properly, set up to the ball as you would like to be at impact.

The Correct Setup

- o When hitting pitch shots inside sixty yards, hold the club a bit shorter with a weak grip.
- o Take an open narrow stance with the left foot turned at a 45° angle and the right foot square to the target line.
- o Sole the club with the face square to the target line and the ball just inside the forward heel.
- o Set your weight on the left side (right-handed player) and the club shaft leaning left. (When looking for a higher loft, you may set up with the ball opposite the instep and the shaft leaning back.)
- o Take it back with an early wrist break forming a 90° angle with the left arm and club shaft and no weight transfer. Keeping the weight on the left side will eliminate swaying and ensuring solid contact.
- o The length of the swing will determine the distance the ball will travel.
- o Swing down and through with hands, arms, and shoulders moving in unison.
- o At impact you want the hands ahead as they were in the address position. Follow these steps and you are on your way to hitting great pitch shots.

Chipping

Chipping is one phase of the game you can master. It does not require great strength nor flexibility as other golf shots require. What you must have are sound fundamentals, willingness to practice, and good imagination to tie it all together. Before making the shot, you must have a plan, a picture in your head. Your aim is to hole the shot or get up and down in two. This is the picture. As part of your routine, you must consider: the slope, the speed of the green, and the distance to the cup.

The club selection can vary from a 6-iron when you face a long uphill chip to a sand iron from in close with little green to work with. As a general rule, always select a club with the least amount of loft to play the shot. I like the ball to carry 20 percent of the distance in the air and 80 percent rolling out to the cup. When you play all the chips in this way, you become very consistent.

The Setup

- o   Once you have determined your line and the landing spot, play from a narrow open stance with the ball back opposite the rear heal.
- o   Shorten down on the club with a weak grip and most of the weight on the forward foot.
- o   The arms and club should form a Y shape with the hands opposite the thigh. You are, with this setup, ready to go.

The Stroke

- o   Relax: get rid of any tension.
- o   The backswing is an upper body move with little to no weight transfer. The wrists will hinge slightly with the shoulders moving as they would when putting.
- o   Unlike putting, the swing through will have the hips and torso turning in unison toward the target.

- The hands at impact are as they were at address with the shaft leaning forward.
- At impact, you want a feel of delofting the club, not adding loft.
- Hold the finish and note that the forward wrist has not cupped, and the clubface is not in a closed position.
- Make practice fun by trying shots from different lies.
- Within your practice session, set a goal of holing a number of chips.
- Master this shot and you are on your way to better golf.

Most, if not all, players have a routine when putting. They are conscious of the break, speed, etc. I do not feel that this is true when playing chips or short pitches to the green. Before playing these shots, walk partway to the hole, and look for breaks in the green, and select the best spot to land the ball. A positive thought such as trying to hole it may help in pulling the shot off to your liking.

Grip Pressure

When practicing shots around the green, experiment with grip pressure for different shots. As a rule, a light grip with weak connection with the club will have the ball release slower and roll less. A tight grip will cause the ball to come off the face faster.

Top left—Here you have a player with a green side chip. When close to the green and playing from a decent lie, go with the least amount of loft to make the shot. This player has a great set up. His weight is left, the ball is back and hands are ahead. The player may use a weak grip or in some cases a putting grip in playing this shot.

Top Right—The player makes a one piece takeaway with a slight hinging of the wrists. The forward swing starts with the knees, hands, arms and shoulders moving in unison.

The left arm, wrist and club are as they were at address. At impact you do not want to add loft to the club. Think hinge and hold through the stroke.

In this picture note the open stance and a target the player hopes to hit. In most cases when chipping you want the ball to have 20% air time and 80% roll to the cup.

The Bump and Run

Knowing how to and when to use the bump and run shot can be a great stroke saver. When playing shots around the green anywhere from the greens' edge to fifty yards out, it is always wise to use the least amount of loft as possible to make the shot. The high lofted shot inside fifty yards is proven to be one of the most difficult shots for most players to perfect. The bump and run will have the ball landing short of the green, bouncing once or twice and rolling out as a putt to the cup. The club selection will depend on the distance to be covered. This shot requires using your imagination. Visualize the ball's flight to the intermediate target and its continued roll out to the cup. Visualizing positive results works. Train yourself to use it!

Key Steps

- Set up as you would for a chip shot, an open stance with the ball just back from center.
- A normal or stronger grip will do, with weight on forward foot.
- Set the hands short on the club with shaft leaning forward.
- Stay steady over the ball (swaying will cause a chunked or topped result), hinge wrists in the backswing; strike down and through maintaining the hinged position, pinching the ball against the turf, taking a thin divot.
- This swing is rotary with the club moving on an inside to inside swing with the club centered in the body.

Here you see the player hitting a bump and run chip to the green. The ball will bounce twice before reaching the green.

Bunker Play—the Fried Egg

The ball in this "fried egg" situation sits partly buried. To extricate the ball from this difficult position, you must use the forward edge of the club to slice down and through the sand under the ball.

Follow these steps:

- Select a 60° wedge, which has less bounce to the sole of the club head.
- Play the ball in the center of the stance and shorten down on the club.
- Lean the shaft forward. This will help the leading edge of the club to dig into the sand.
- Picture the swing you want to make as a V-shaped swing.
- This swing is more of an upper body swing with the weight on the forward foot throughout the swing.
- Swing the club back and down at a steep angle, striking the sand an inch or two behind the ball and finish low.
- You can expect the ball to come out fairly low with little to zero backspin.

Bunker Play

When playing from a green side bunker, the lie of the ball and the texture of the sand will determine how you play the shot and which club to select.

Playing from a Flat Lie and Dry Sand to a Close Pin

- Select a sand iron of 56°-58° or 60° degree of loft.
- Take an open stance with the ball left of center and the club face open to the target.
- In the down swing keep the weight left striking three to four inches behind the ball.
- With this action, you will hit high soft shots that will settle down nicely on the green.

Left—This is the set up from a green side bunker. Note that the hands are even with the clubhead.

Right—In making the backswing and downswing, keep the clubhead just outside the hands.

The player has struck the sand 3 to 4 inches behind the ball. He has taken a shallow divot and notice that the club face has not closed.

Playing from a Firm Wet Bunker

- You will have better results when playing this shot using a club with less bounce to the sole.
- Take an open stance with the ball just left of center and weight centered.
- Take a normal grip, shorten down on the club, and lean the shaft forward allowing the forward edge of the club to dig into the soil.
- When playing this shot keep the weight on the forward side. This shot requires taking a shallow divot striking an inch or two behind the ball.

Downhill Bunker Shot

- Club of choice—60° wedge.
- Set up open to the intended line with shoulders, when possible, parallel to the slope.
- Position the ball right of center with weight on the forward foot.
- Make an upright backswing with a quick wrist lock.
- Slide the knees down the slope, and slide the club under the ball, and keep the club moving down the slope.

The player in this set-up (Down Hill Bunker shot) has his weight to the left, hands ahead, ball position back and the club face open. From this position he is able to slide the club head down the slope taking a thin divot out from under the ball.

Fairway Bunker Shot

First and foremost, select a club with enough loft to clear the lip of the bunker. Don't be greedy. Getting the ball back in play is more important than the distance.

- Take an open stance; work your feet into the sand for a solid footing.
- Shorten down on the club an inch or two.
- Play the ball in the center, assuring clean contact with the ball.

When playing from sand, take note of the lie and texture of the sand since the situation you're in will determine the club selection. As a general rule from firm or wet sand, select a club with little bounce to the sole, and strike close to the ball. Playing from soft dry sand requires a standard sand iron striking two to three inches behind the ball.

The Hybrid from Fairway Bunkers

The hybrid with its wide sole and low center of gravity would be a good choice of club from fairway bunkers. Set up with a good footing and the ball just left of center. Make a shorter, flatter than normal backswing and a shallow attack angle to the ball. When desiring less distance from the bunker, merely hold the club shorter.

When playing from a fairway bunker be sure to have a solid footing. Play the ball in the center of the stance with your hands over the ball. Hold the club a bit shorter to insure a clean contact to the ball.

Uphill Bunker Play

The Setup

- Set your weight on the back foot and an open stance.
- Shoulders parallel to the slope and ball just left of center.
- Shorten down on the club with the clubface square.
- The uphill lie will cause the ball to come out higher.
- Take a thin divot, and swing hard enough to advance the ball to the target

SECTION 5

Select the Right Club 85
Use The Right Wedge 86
One-Arm Drill 87
Creating Backspin 88
The Flop Shot 89
Play From Green Side Rough 90
Playing From Hard Pan 92

Select the Right Club

When playing to the green from inside one hundred yards, take note of the flags' position. The club you select can determine the score you are likely to make. With the flag close to the front, the more lofted wedge would be the choice. With the flag up back, the less lofted wedge will do the job. When in doubt as to which wedge to use, always go with the less lofted one and swing within yourself.

The wedges in your bag are the scoring clubs. When playing wedge shots to the green; make short compact swings for more consistency. There is no need to look for extra distance with these short clubs.

Use The Right Wedge

When pitching from a close cut fairway, your choice of club should be a wedge with little bounce or a pitching wedge with no bounce. The opposite choice from a soft lie or light rough would be a wedge with a greater degree of bounce.

One-Arm Drill

This is a one-arm drill, both right and left that John Daly, one of golf's great short-game players incorporates into his practice routine.

If you are looking to improve those important short shots from around the green, then you must add this drill to your practice session.

When practicing this chipping drill take your normal set up but with the forward hand only. The simplest and most efficient way to chip is to hinge the wrist in the back swing and hold the position through impact. The one arm drill will force you to maintain the hinge position since you do not have the support of your other hand.

When hitting longer pitch shots from ten to forty yards, hinge the wrist making a 90° angle with left arm and club. Swing through at impact again keeping the left arm and club as they were at address.

This drill will keep you from adding loft to the club and scooping the ball at impact.

Creating Backspin

All golf shots that stay airborne have some degree of backspin. The tour players and low handicappers, because of their clubhead speed and ability to make solid contact, do put a great deal of spin to the ball. Good swing mechanics will result in a clean solid contact of the ball generating the backspin needed to keep the ball from advancing too far upon hitting the green.

The equipment and type of ball in use will also influence the ball's capacity to spin. For more spin;

- Play a softer-covered ball, and with the short clubs 9-iron through lob wedge, play the ball center or back.
- Stay centered over the ball, stance open, with 60 percent of the weight on the forward foot.
- With a slight out-to-in swing plane, strike the ball cleanly taking a thin divot and little release of the club.
- Be certain that the grooves are clear of grass and soil.
- It may be wise to purchase new and up-to-date wedges after two or three years of use.

The Flop Shot

The flop shot can be a great bail-out shot. It does, however, require a great deal of practice and a shot you are not apt to use often.

The suggested club is a 56°, 58°, or 60° lofted wedge with little bounce to the sole.

In the setup, weaken your grip, V shapes to your chin, take a wider stance aiming a bit left of the target with a bit more weight on the back foot. Position the ball a bit left of center with the clubface slightly opened to the target. Set the hands a bit lower and back from the clubhead

Stay steady over the ball with very little weight transfer. Make an early wrist cock, cupping the left wrist, ensuring an open club face. Start the downswing with the shoulders arms and hands moving in unison. Slide the club under the ball. Finish with a bit more weight on the rear foot with the clubface to the sky. This shot requires a great deal of practice but is a very rewarding shot to have in the bag.

Play From Green Side Rough

One of the most difficult shots in golf is playing from heavy rough with little green to work with. This shot requires a great deal of practice and with practice comes confidence and success.

As Gary Player said, "The more I practice the luckier I get." So to get "luckier," try the following:

- Select a lob wedge of 60° with little bounce.
- This shot is similar to playing from a bunker. Hold the club a bit shorter, take an open stance, and play the ball just inside the forward foot.
- The backswing will require a quick setting of the wrists.
- The downswing should be on a steep angle, eliminating as much grass as possible between clubface and ball.
- The follow-through should be short with the clubface open and the club and left forearm in line as in the setup.
- Take a few practice swings before attempting the shot. Picture the desired results.

When playing from light rough around the greens try the hybrid club. With its wide sole and low center of gravity you may have better results than using a more lofted club.

Playing From Hard Pan

What makes this shot so difficult, for professionals and amateur players alike, is the fact that due to the firm soil you are not able to slide the club head under the ball. In any case, when playing a full shot or one close to the green, the ball must be struck with a descending blow, striking the ball first and pinching it against the soil.

In the setup, shorten down on the club a bit with the ball just back of center with your weight forward. For best results select a club with little flange to the sole.

This player is in an ideal position when playing off hard pan.

SECTION 6

Saving Strokes 97
Play To the Middle of the Green 98
The Par Threes 99
Uneven Lies 100

Saving Strokes

In order to lower your handicap, you must know how to save strokes. First and foremost, you must know the weaknesses in your game and, with that, make the necessary improvements. For example, if you have difficulty hitting drives to narrow fairways, then select the 3 or 5 fairway metal from the tee; hit the shots you know you can make. Play a lay-up shot when in doubt about carrying a shot, over water or a bunker, to the green. When hitting to the green, play to the safe side of the flag. You will be well served spending most of your practice time from inside one hundred yards. I find that the approach shots to the green that require imagination and feel is where most amateur players are lacking.

Play To the Middle of the Green

Unless you are an amateur champion or a tour player, you want to avoid going for the flags. Your chances of making par or better when hitting a full shot to the green is to aim at the center of the green.

The tour average on full shots to the pin is about thirty-one feet. When you aim to the center of the green, you will hit more greens, have fewer three-putts, and make more birdies.

The Par Threes

Par threes are the most difficult holes to par. You get one shot at hitting the green where on a par four, you have two shots to the green; and on the fives, which are the easiest to par, you get three shots to reach the green. Always tee the ball when playing the par threes, take enough club and play to the center of the green.

Uneven Lies

Golf courses are not flat, and as any golfer knows, the ball will settle in some strange places. With changes to the set up and swing adjustments, you can overcome odd lies and get the ball to the target.

Downhill Lie

The Stance

- Take a swing or two and notice where the club bottoms out. In most cases, it will be back of center.
- Set your weight on the forward leg, and select a club with more loft, that is, if the shot calls for a 6-iron to reach the green select a number 7.
- This shot will normally move to the right or slice a bit, so aim a bit left for a right hand player.
- To keep from topping this shot, set the shoulders parallel to slope, and stay steady over the ball with the shaft perpendicular to the ground. Swing the club down the slope, and finish with a low follow through.

A severe downhill lie is one of the toughest shots in golf. When playing this shot, always go with a more lofted iron and avoid fairway woods. Maintaining your balance is your first priority.

Uphill Lie

- Take a swing or two and notice where the club bottoms out. In most cases, it will be a bit left of center.
- Set the weight a bit to the forward foot (with a severe uphill lie, the weight would be more to the rear leg) and shoulders parallel to the ground.
- In most cases when playing from an uphill lie your best bet is to take more club.
- Balance is the key in making this shot.

Side Hill Lies with Ball Below your Feet

The Stance

- o Bend at the waist and flex the knees. Keep your rear back so that you do not fall forward during the swing.
- o Take a swing or two and notice where the club bottoms out. In most cases, it is in the center of your stance.
- o From this lie, the ball will go right or slice due to a more upright swing plane. From this setup, the backswing will be limited, so take extra clubs to get the desired distance.

Side Hill Lie with Ball Above your Feet

The Stance

- o Stand taller; take a swing or two, and notice where the club bottoms out. In most cases, you will play the ball center or back a bit to lessen the hook.
- o Hold the club shorter since the ball is up closer to you.
- o A shot from this lie tends to go to the left, so aim a bit right and maintain good balance throughout the swing.
- o This swing will feel a bit like a baseball swing. From this lie, you can expect the ball flight to be lower and roll out longer when it strikes the ground. Proper posture and balance are key to successfully executing these shots.

SECTION 7

The Driver	105
The Takeaway	110
The Impact Zone	114
Clubhead Lag	116
Transition—Back To Down	119
The Long Irons	120
Golf And Baseball	121
Swing Through To The Finish	122

The Driver

The driver is one of three clubs in your bag that I refer to as the "big three" the other two are the pitching wedge (or sand iron) and of course the putter. Today's golf has become a power game. The average player is driving the ball longer than anyone could have imagined just a few years ago. There are several reasons for this. Primarily, the advances in technology and that the world's best players are stronger, more physical, and more knowledgeable of the swing mechanics.

To get more distance in order to stay up with your fellow competitors off the tee, try the following setup with the driver:

- o   Tee the ball higher; three-fourths of the ball above the top edge of the clubhead
- o   For more clubhead speed, stand an inch or two further away from the ball.
- o   Play the ball opposite the forward instep.
- o   Feet shoulder width, flare the forward foot out to a 45° angle. This will allow you to rotate the hips faster through impact.
- o   Knees flexed, push your butt out, and belt buckle tilted toward the target line.
- o   The spine wants to be tilted back with 60 percent of the weight on the rear foot.

This setup will allow you to make a flatter swing around your body and a shallow attack angle to the ball.

For added yards;

- o   Eliminate tension from hands, arms, and shoulders.
- o   Make a wide backswing and full shoulder turn, with arms relaxed and the forward arm extended but not rigid.

JOHN OTERI

- At the completion of the back swing, you want the right knee as it was at address.
- On the downswing picture the club moving through the ball, not at the ball, on an inside to inside swing plane with full extension of the arms. Finish with your weight on your forward foot, your knees close together, hips facing the target and chest facing left of target through to a full balanced finish.

(See "Swing Through to the Finish" in this Section)

Here you see a great set-up, grip, stance, posture. Note the tilt of the shoulders due to the spine tilt to the right. This tilt puts a bit more weight to the back foot. Note also the hands are over the clubhead not the ball. From this sound position the player is set to launch the ball a long way.

In the backswing we like to see the shoulder to the ball or beyond and back to the target. Due to age and limited flexibility not everyone can get into the position of this player but we should try to get to our maximum backswing rotation.

For maximum launch angle you want at least 50% of the balls diameter above the clubhead.

The Takeaway

The takeaway at the start of the swing is an upper body move. There is no one way to start the swing, and you will notice that when watching the tour players, some will start from a static position and others with a waggle of the club and a forward press, where the hands move a bit toward the target to initiate the backswing. One is just as good as the other. What you don't want are overactive hands where the club is picked up too soon, eliminating a proper rotation and weight transfer. The golf swing is on an inclined plane controlled by the hands and arms, along with the shoulder rotation, setting the club on plane.

- First and foremost, the player must have the proper setup and alignment to the target.
- A one-piece start (right-handed player) will have hands, arms, and shoulders (shoulders will feel as moving horizontally) moving in unison.
- The wrists will begin to hinge once they pass the rear thigh.
- When the hands are waist high, the left arm will be horizontal to the ground and parallel to the target line.
- The butt of the club at this point is pointing at the target line.
- This is a great start to the swing with the hands and arms continuing in an upward plane to the top of the backswing.
- The player is now in a good position to start the downswing.

The golf swing starts with an upper body move—that is, with hands, arms, and shoulders. The downswing starts with a lower body move—that is, feet, knees, and hips; amateurs make a major mistake in starting the downswing with the hands. Once at the top of your backswing, be patient; no one is going to take the ball away. Start the downswing from the feet up.

Half way back in the swing an ideal position is when the toe of the club is skyward and the club is parallel to the target line.

Left—This player has the club in a good position with left arm extension and the club face parallel to the forearm.

Right—Note in this position the left wrist is cupped with the toe of the club down. From this open position of the club face the player most likely will slice right of the target.

In this position the player has a bowed or convex wrist with the club face to the sky. From this position the shot will most likely go low and left of the target.

The Impact Zone

The most important section of the golf swing is the impact zone, when the clubhead is eighteen inches approaching impact to eighteen inches beyond impact. All the great ball strikers are in the so-called correct zone no matter how the swing looked on its way to the zone. When you watch Jim Furyk, Ernie Els or Fred Couples, you see three different swings, but on impact, they all appear to be the same. In order to have the clubhead square at impact, you must;

- Have the club moving on an inside approach to the ball.
- Keep the upper rear arm close to the rib cage.
- The forward wrist should be flat or slightly bowed.
- The forward leg at impact will be straightening up, carrying most of the weight with the hips tuned half way to the target.

Impact Tape

Today's high-tech equipment has the tour players hitting the ball much farther than ever. The other factor to consider is that tour players strike the ball in the center or sweet spot on the clubface. Most amateurs do not. I would suggest using impact tape that will show impact areas on the clubface. Once you have that information, you can then make the necessary changes to improve your ball striking.

At impact, you see this player in an ideal impact position. Note that his weight is forward, hips partially open to the target and the right knee moving left. The arms are extended and the hands and arms are where they were at address with the hands forward of the ball. Notice that this player is practicing with a glove under the left arm. At impact you want the upper left arm close to the rib cage. This position insures good contact and eliminates a chicken wing action of the left arm.

Clubhead Lag

Clubhead lag is the result of the player starting the downswing with the lower body, allowing the hands to lead the club down. The result is the bowing of the shaft as the clubhead trails. Poor ball striking is the result of moving and releasing the hands and wrist cock too soon, resulting in the hands behind the ball at impact.

Well-struck golf shots will have the hands and shaft forward of the clubhead at impact.

Try this drill:

Stop at the top of your backswing. Start the downswing slowly and stop when your hands are opposite the rear foot. At this point in your swing, your wrists should still be cocked and the angle of wrist and shaft are at 90° or greater. As the hands and body rotation accelerate, the clubhead remains in a lag position.

Stop at impact with the club behind the ball, and notice if you did this drill correctly, the hands should be ahead of the clubhead.

To eliminate the disastrous over-the-top move causing a hook, slice or topped shot, keep the rear shoulder back and down as you start the downswing.

Here you see the player with hands waist high in the down swing. Make note that the right elbow is close to the side, wrists fully cocked and the butt end of the club is to the target line. This is an ideal position that you should practice.

The through swing should mirror the down swing. With the release of the hands and rotation of the arms. The butt end of the club will point to the target line in the follow through.

Transition — Back To Down

This is a critical motion in the golf swing. For a smooth transition, realize first that you want to swing through the ball, not at the ball. Quick hands at the start of the downswing is a major reason for poor ball striking. Try the following:

- Start with a lower body move as you would in throwing a ball. This will set in motion the proper lower body move delaying the hands and arms.
- Turning the hips with a bump and turn will put the club on the proper plane and help eliminate the over-the-top move.
- A feel of leaving the clubhead motionless at the top of the swing for a very brief moment, as Kenny Perry and Ernie Els do, will lead to the proper transition from back to down.

The Long Irons

Jack Nicklaus was a great long iron player who never felt it necessary to overpower the longer irons instead he swung them like he would a 7-iron.

For more success with these clubs, try the following:

- Play the ball just inside the left heel for a high ball flight and just left of center for a lower flight.
- The swing plane should be more rounded or flatter to make an inside and shallow attack angle to the ball.
- At impact, the hands should be even with the club head or a bit behind.
- Stay tall through the shot to avoid taking a deep divot.
- Maintain good balance throughout the swing.
- Most golfers have a hybrid or two in there bag. The hybrid with its wide sole and lower center of gravity will get the ball airborne much easier than the long iron. For best results when playing the hybrid be sure to play the ball as you would with an iron as mentioned above and don't attempt to sweep the ball from the fairway.

Golf And Baseball

One is a horizontal swing; the other, an upright swing. At impact in both swings, the forward arm is extended, the rear arm inflexed with the elbow close to the hip, the forward leg is straight, the head back, and hips turning toward the target. The release has the rear hand rotating over the forward hand.

I highly recommend that you add the baseball swing—that is, swinging the club, with relaxed hands and arms horizontally, back and through, creating as much sound as you can as the club cuts through the air. With this drill, you will feel the correct release of the hands resulting in more clubhead speed and distance.

Many years ago I witnessed Mickey Mantle and Jim Rice driving balls well over three hundred yards carry with wood head clubs. What would they do with today's high tech drivers?

Swing Through To The Finish

Failing to finish the swing you started will result in loss of distance and misdirected shots.

When watching tour players, you will notice how they hold the finish in some cases until the ball has landed. With a full balanced finish, you can expect maximum clubhead speed and better direction to your shots. Attempting to steer the ball with a shorter swing will result in loss of distance and direction.

A full finish must have:

1. perfect balance,
2. weight on forward foot,
3. knees close together,
4. hips to or slightly left of target,
5. shoulders left of target, and
6. hands over left shoulder.

Due to age or flexibility issues, we can't all expect to look like tour players, but we should strive to make the fullest swing possible.

Section 8

The Quick Hook 125
The Draw 126
The Slice 127
The Fade 128
The Topped Shot 129
Split Grip 130

The Quick Hook

The quick or duck hook is the one shot you cannot play golf with. You can get away with a slice since it will not run into as much trouble as the duck hook. I like the phrase, "You can talk to a fade, but a hook won't listen."

Poor basics are the major reason for the hook such as;

- A grip that is too strong with the hands turned too far right (right-handed player), with three or more knuckles showing on the back of the left hand,
- Alignment that is too far to the right of the target with a closed stance,
- A club that is not soled properly—toe of the club off the ground,
- Attempting to hit the ball too hard, and
- Overactive hands and upper body.

Any of the above will cause the clubface to be closed at impact imparting a counterclockwise spin to the ball.

A Cure

- Improve your basics—grip, stance, alignment, and posture.
- The backswing is an upper body move and downswing a lower body move.
- Be patient and swing the club. Don't hit at the ball.
- Set the club at the top of the backswing with a slight pause before starting the downswing allowing the lower body, feet, legs, and hips to kick in.
- Picture at impact the hips clearing, hands ahead of the clubhead, and right elbow close to the right side.
- Practice with these thoughts in mind, and you are on your way to better golfing.

The Draw

The draw (right-handed player) is a shot that has a subtle right-to-left ball flight unlike a hook. This is a great shot to have in your arsenal when you must shape a shot on a dog leg left hole, into wind, or around a tree, etc.

Making this shot does not require a swing change but a setup change.

The Draw Setup

- Take your normal grip.
- Set the clubface in line to the target.
- Adjust your feet, hips, and shoulders to the right of the target.
- The degree that your setup is in relation to your target line will determine the amount of draw.
- With a normal swing from this position, the club will move on an in to out swing path. Pronating of the hands and arms will apply a counterclockwise action to the ball.
- Golf is more fun when you can work the ball at will, so get out there and give it a try.

The Slice

The dreaded slice for a right-handed player (opposite for left-handed player) has the ball moving clockwise, left to right. Anyone who has played the game knows the feeling, and it is not a pretty one. There are various degrees of a slice based on the loft of the club and the speed with which the ball leaves the clubface. As a rule, the longer less-lofted clubs will create more of a slice than the shorter more-lofted clubs. A ball can only move left to right due to being struck from right to left. Once you understand the cause, then you can work on counter moves.

I recommend that you develop good basics starting with the grip and study in this section how to draw and hook the ball.

The Fade

The "Fade", for a right hand player is one that moves left of the target as it comes off the club face. As a result of the clockwise spin applied to the ball, the ball will move to the right as it descends on the target. A change in the alignment to the target, not a swing change, will result in the desired ball flight.

The Set Up;

- Set the clubhead to the target.
- Take an open stance, feet, knees, shoulders aligned left and be sure the clubface remains on line to the target as you make these adjustments.
- Making a normal swing with this set up will cause a glancing strike to the ball.
- When desiring a greater degree of fade align further left of the target.

The fade is played by most of the tour players and was the desired ball flight for Jack Nicklous, Lee Trevino and the great Ben Hogan.

The Topped Shot

The topped shot or the thin hit is basically the same with the club striking the ball at or above the equator. In any case, the results of this action are unpredictable.

There are several factors relating to a topped shot and the way you hold the club is not an issue.

Possible Causes

- A poor setup aiming too far left or right, making good contact difficult.
- A backswing that is too flat or too upright.
- A sway where the weight moves to the outside of the back foot.
- Dropping your head in the backswing will then pull up in the downswing
- A reverse pivot where the body weight leans forward in the backswing and backward in the downswing.
- At impact, the left or forward arm is not extended but bent and pulling up in a chicken-wing fashion.

As you can see, if you do have an issue with topping, you have a lot of work to do.

You cannot get away from basic fundamentals in setup, posture, and balance throughout the swing.

Split Grip

Try the split grip drill for better contact with the ball. Topping the ball, mishit shots, and left-to-right shots are generally the result of a poor release. Try this drill with the right hand below the left make a few half to three quarter swings. You will notice in the backswing a greater degree of wrist cock and the right arm folding to the proper position. Swinging through impact, you will feel a different sensation as the hands release with a powerful move of the right hand, striking down and through. After a few swings with the split grip, go back to your normal grip and hit balls with the same feel you had with the split grip. Add this drill to your practice sessions, and you will make better contact with the ball.

SECTION 9

Purposeful Practice 133
Drive It Low 135
Hit It Low From the Fairway 136
The Release 137
Right Knee Flex 138
A Higher Ball Flight 139
Get an Overhaul 140

Purposeful Practice

When you step on the practice tee, you must have an objective and concentrate on achieving that objective. It is very difficult and time consuming to make real and everlasting swing changes. Once you're certain of the objective, it is best to concentrate on that one issue in each practice session. This is the best way to ingrain the new move into your swing.

The pace of your practice session is an important factor. Be patient. Follow the flight of each ball; pause and reflect on the results of that shot. It may be a good idea to position the practice balls a few yards away from the hitting station as a way of slowing down.

The most common hitting station is merely placing two clubs on the ground as a railroad track aimed to your target. A row of tees or a third club lying perpendicular to your target line will help with ball position.

During the session, take note of the divots. The direction of the divots will show the swing plane. The depth of the divot will also reveal swing faults. Take note that divots going left of the target, the most common result for the average golfers, are the results of an out-to-in swing, resulting in a pull or sliced shot. A divot going to the right of the target is caused by an in-to-out swing path resulting in a push, slice, or hook. A deep divot resulting in a fat shot and loss on distance may be the result of overuse of the hands or poor weight transfer in the downswing. When you have an understanding of your swing faults and your practice sessions are not bearing results, then it is time to see your local golf professional.

Once you have developed a consistent swing, you can then add shot making to your practice sessions. Shot making techniques hitting it low, high left or right at will. It is fun to practice all kinds of shots from various lies and positions. As you know, the ball can come to rest in some unbelievable places.

Avoid practicing from mats when possible. Due to the firmness of mats, the shafts can bend at the hosel and graphite shafts may splinter.

Drive It Low

Setup and swing plane are key when you want to drive it low into the wind or to take advantage of a hard and fast fairway. As in making all golf shots, part of your routine is to picture the shot before swinging the club. This does help to get the desired results. In the setup, tee the ball a bit lower and take a flatter swing plane, set your shoulder's level and picture a baseball-type swing.

In the downswing, you want the club approaching the ball at a shallow angle of attack. At impact, feel that you are covering the ball with the upper body, taking the ball cleanly off the tee with a lower finish with hands over the left shoulder and left elbow down toward the left hip.

Hit It Low From the Fairway

For most golfers, playing in windy conditions becomes quite a challenge.

Hitting it low is not as difficult as it seems. With the proper setup and minor swing changes in execution, you will be able to hit it low at will.

The Setup

Take a normal grip, shorten down, and take more club.

Narrow the stance, and play the ball back from center. This will set your hands ahead and de-loft the club. As part of your pre shot routine, picture a shorter, more compact swing on a flatter swing plane. The shallow flatter plane will reduce the back spin and cause the ball to fly lower.

The Release

The release is basically keeping the clubface square from start to finish. For a powerful release, try this drill:

o   Hold the club; don't grip it.
o   Swing the club as you would a baseball bat.
o   Notice how the right hand releases over the left. Keep the hands and arms relaxed as you swing, and notice the increase in clubhead speed as you turn your hips to an open position allowing the clubhead to remain back, then releasing the arms and hands to the finish.
o   Repeat the drill, and notice how the right arm rotates over the left through the hitting area. Notice how the upper left and right arm remains close to the body with this drill

Right Knee Flex

Maintaining the right knee flex from setup to impact is critical to good ball striking. Straightening the right knee in the backswing may cause a reverse pivot or topped shot. For balance and to eliminate a sway the right knee and leg must remain stable.

Lee Trevino, one of golf's greatest ball strikers, advocated the use of the right knee and leg as a great power source at the start of the downswing.

A Higher Ball Flight

A high ball flight is the desired flight when hitting to a tight pin placement over trees, hazards, etc.

When it is necessary to hit it high, try the following method:

o   It will help to think high. The body does react to what the mind and subconscious wish it to do.
o   In the setup, align the ball just inside the forward heel.
o   Standing closer to the ball will cause a more upright swing.
o   Set a bit more weight to the back foot and keep your hands back from the clubhead.

Get an Overhaul

No matter what your handicap, if golf is your passion, you owe it to yourself to have your swing looked at once or twice a year by a qualified PGA teacher. The world's best players are constantly working on the basics under the watchful eye of a coach. It is the little things in golf that can go astray such as alignment, grip, stance, posture, and ball position. Get with it and check it out with your local PGA golf professional.

Made in the USA
Lexington, KY
27 January 2012